A New True Book

TALKING BIRDS

By Alice K. Flanagan

Subject Consultant
David E. Willard, Ph.D.
Collection Manager of Birds at the Field Museum
of Natural History, Chicago, Illinois

Children's Press®
A Division of Grolier Publishing
New York   London   Hong Kong   Sydney
Danbury, Connecticut

The New Zealand kea is an unusual parrot.

For all those who love to talk to birds

PHOTO CREDITS

Animals, Animals — © Fritz Prenzel, cover, 32, 35 (left); © E. R. Degginger, 4 (top), 17 (left); © Hans & Judy Beste, 6; © Noah Satat, 8; © Michael Fogden, 10 (left); © Ron Willocks, 10 (right); © Stephen Dalton, 17 (right), 21 (left); © Patti Murray, 21 (right); © John Chellman, 23 (left), 34 (right); © George X. Bryce, 23 (right); © Gerard Lacz, 25 (top right); © John Pontier, 25 (bottom right); © Ken Cole, 26; © Robert Maier, 28; © Reed/Williams, 29 (top left); © Jim Tuten, 31 (left); © Tony Tilford, 34 (left); © Mickey Gibson, 35 (right)

Jeff Foott Productions — © Jeff Foott, 4 (bottom), 25 (top left)

Valan Photos — © John Cancalosi, 2, 25 (bottom left); © Rob Simpson, 7 (left), 13, 37; © Stephen J. Krasemann, 7 (right), 14; © Pam E. Hickman, 18 (top); © Kennon Cooke, 18 (bottom), 45; © K. Gant, 29 (top right); © Tom W. Parkin, 29 (bottom); © Jean-Marie Jro, 31 (right); © M. J. Johnson, 39; © Herman H. Giethoorn, 41; © J. R. Page, 42

COVER: Rainbow lorikeet from Australia

Project Editor: Dana Rau
Electronic Composition: Biner Design
Photo Research: Flanagan Publishing Services

Library of Congress Cataloging-in-Publication Data

Flanagan, Alice.
    Talking Birds / by Alice K. Flanagan.
        p. cm. — (A New true book)
    Includes index.
    Summary: Highlights a variety of parrots, mynah birds, and other birds that can talk.
    ISBN 0-516-01096-4
    1. Parrots—Juvenile literature. 2. Mynahs—Juvenile literature. 3. Talking birds—Juvenile literature. [1. Parrots. 2. Mynahs. 3. Talking birds.] I. Title.
QL696.P7F57 1996   95-43801
636.6'865—dc20   CIP   AC

CONTENTS

Can Birds Really Talk? . . . 5

How Do Birds Communicate? . . . 9

The Best Talking Birds . . . 16

African Grays and Amazons . . . 20

Macaws . . . 24

Budgies and Parakeets . . . 27

Cockatoos and Cockatiels . . . 30

Lories and Lorikeets . . . 34

Mynahs . . . 36

Teaching Birds to Talk . . . 38

Glossary . . . 46

Index . . . 48

About the Author . . . 48

(Above) The brilliant red lorikeet is a member of the parrot family.
(Left) Macaws of Central and South America are the largest parrots.

CAN BIRDS REALLY TALK?

Listen to a parrot sing a popular song. Answer a mynah bird when it asks you a question. Think about what you've just heard. Can birds really talk?

From studying birds, we know that all birds communicate. They call, chatter, and sing. Some even imitate, or mimic, sounds. The superb lyrebird of Australia, for example, has been heard imitating the squeal of a pig, the howl of a dog, and even the sounds of farm machinery. But very few birds have the ability to mimic human sounds.

Parrots and some starlings can imitate

The superb lyrebird of Australia mimics other birds' songs and imitates sounds.

(Left) Crows are intelligent birds.
They can be tamed and taught human
speech.
(Above) Starlings are very sociable.
Many are good mimics.

human speech. However,
we do not know if they
understand what they are
saying. This does not
mean that birds are not
smart. They are very

Like starlings and lyrebirds, the crested lark imitates sounds.

capable of using their own sounds to communicate with us. Perhaps one day we will prove that some birds can understand and use our words to communicate with us.

HOW DO BIRDS COMMUNICATE?

Birds use sounds to communicate. They produce a great variety of calls to pass along information about the location of food and enemies, or predators. They also use calls to keep in contact with members of their group.

Some calls are instinctive, which means

(Left) The three-wattled bellbird of Costa Rica has a loud bell-like call.
(Above) The calls for food of recently hatched northern mockingbirds are instinctive.

they do not have to be learned. A hungry baby bird, for example, does not have to be taught to beg for food from its parents. It instinctively cries for food. It also reacts instinctively to parents' alarm calls about predators in the area.

Many bird calls are learned. Birds that live in groups often use calls to let members of the group know where they are. These are contact calls. Before birds leave a feeding flock and fly to another spot, they usually make a contact call to the others. Then, the others follow. If one member is left behind, it will search for the flock, calling loudly until it finds the other birds.

Another way birds communicate is with chatter. Unlike contact calls, which are short loud bursts, courtship or mate chatter includes soft notes voiced by an adult male and female. Mated parakeets often cuddle and coo quietly, or chatter to each other.

Singing is also a way of communicating. Among songbirds, a baby starling will imitate the sounds it hears from adult singers of its species, just as a human

Monk
parakeets

child imitates the sounds it
hears spoken in its family.
Once a song is learned, it is
used to identify territory,
keep in contact with a mate
and offspring, and warn
intruders to stay away.

Red and yellow
barbets of east
Africa keep in
touch with each
other by songs
and calls.

Paired or mated birds use
calls and songs to stay in
touch with each other at a
distance. Some mates learn
each others' unique calls
and songs. When they are

14

together, each sings a
part of the song. This is
called duetting. When the
same pair is apart, each
repeats the song until the
mate returns.

Perhaps this is what
parrots and mynahs are
doing when they mimic
humans. They may be
trying to link themselves to
their owners and remind
them of their presence.
"Look, here I am," they
may be saying. "I'm
talking to you!"

THE BEST
TALKING BIRDS

Most parrots and some starlings are among the best imitators of the human voice. These birds do not mimic humans in the wild. In captivity, however, many can be trained to repeat human sounds. The greater hill mynah is by far the most gifted speaker in the starling family. The

The Indian hill mynah (left) and the African gray parrot (right)

African gray is the finest in
the parrot family.

Like songbirds, parrots
and mynah birds have a
highly developed organ
for making sounds. It is
called a syrinx, and it is
located at the base of the

17

Parrots
African Gray
Amazons
Budgies
Cockatiels
Cockatoos
Lories and Lorikeets
Macaws
Parakeets (Conures)

Mynahs

Bald	Greater Hill
Common	House
Crested	Indian Hill
Golden-Crested	Javan Hill
	Lesser Hill

throat, or trachea. Parrots also have large, thick tongues that aid them in turning the sounds made by the syrinx into speech.

When raised properly in captivity, parrots and mynahs can be wonderful companions. Most are affectionate and easily trained. They can provide a world of enjoyment for a long time. Some birds have been known to live as long as eighty years.

AFRICAN GRAYS AND AMAZONS

The African gray parrot is one of the best-known parrots in the world. Ancestors of the African gray came from west and central Africa. They get their name from their ash-gray color. They are very affectionate birds and the most talented talkers of their species.

(Above) African grays have bright red tails.
(Right) The Cayman Amazon on the left and the yellow-fronted Amazon on the right are mainly green.

Amazons are one of the most popular groups of parrots. Although they are named after a river that flows through South America, these birds are also common throughout Central America and some of the Caribbean Islands.

Amazons are mainly green. There are color differences, however, on the forehead, crown, and cheek areas. Variations in size also help to tell them apart.

The double yellow-head is the most popular of the Amazons. Its name refers to the size its head becomes when it gets excited.

The yellow-naped Amazon is green from head to tail, except for a slightly yellow color on the tips of the tail feathers. About a

A yellow-naped parrot (left) and a yellow-headed parrot (right)

year after birth, yellow-
napes develop a bright
yellow patch on the nape,
or back of the neck.
Among the Amazons, the
yellow-napes are the most
tame and the best talkers.

MACAWS

Macaws are the largest of parrots. They come from Central and South America. For generations, native people have used macaw feathers to decorate their clothing and homes. The hyacinth macaw is the largest of all the parrots. It is a gentle and friendly bird.

A blue and yellow macaw (top left), military macaw (top right),
hyacinth macaw (bottom left), and scarlet macaw (bottom right)

A scarlet macaw from Central America

Some people say that Christopher Columbus brought the first macaws from the New World back to Spain.

BUDGIES AND PARAKEETS

The budgie, or budgerigar, may be the most popular pet bird in the world. This small, clever bird originally came from Australia. It is a member of a larger group called parakeets.

Budgies come in a wonderful variety of colors — blue, green, white, and

You can tell if an adult budgie is male or female by the color of the skin above its nostrils. Male skin is bluish. Female skin is brownish. Can you find the males and females in this photo?

yellow. Once tamed, they make good speakers.

Parakeets, or conures, come from South America, Central America, and Mexico. They are very different than budgies. They act more like true parrots. They vary greatly

A sun conure (top left), rose-ringed parakeet (top right), and red-crowned parakeet (left)

in color, markings, and size. Although they are limited in talking ability, parakeets are clever, loving birds and easily tamed.

COCKATOOS AND COCKATIELS

Cockatoos are highly intelligent parrots, but they are not great talkers. They come from Australia, New Zealand, and the surrounding islands of the South Pacific. They are known for their playfulness and great sense of curiosity. Among the cockatoos, the moluccans

A moluccan cockatoo (left)
and galah cockatoo (above)

are considered one of the
best talkers. As if aware of
their beauty, cockatoos will
often toss their head back,
raise the crest, and proudly
display their wings.

31

Cockatiels belong to the same family as cockatoos. In fact, they behave much like "mini" cockatoos. They are gray but have white markings across their wings and yellow and orange areas on their faces. Cockatiels also have a little crest on top of their heads. They can be taught to talk and whistle.

A pair of cockatiels

LORIES AND LORIKEETS

This family of small parrots from Australia is known for its shiny brilliant feathers. Lories have short tails. Lorikeets have long tails. Unlike other parrots, these birds have hairs at the end of their tongues. They use these brushlike tongues to lick flower nectar and pollen. The rainbow lorikeet is a popular bird from this group.

A yellow-backed lory (opposite page, left), a chattering lory (opposite page, right), a red-collared lorikeet (below left), and a rainbow lorikeet (below right)

MYNAHS

Mynahs belong to the
starling family and are
native to India, Burma, and
many other parts of Asia.
These shiny black birds
can imitate human speech
better than parrots can.

The two most popular
talking mynahs are the
greater hill mynah and the
lesser hill mynah. Many

The coleto mynah is one of several outstanding mimics in the starling family.

consider the greater hill to be the finest of all talking birds. Although its voice is rather loud and harsh, it becomes quite beautiful when imitating the songs of other birds.

TEACHING BIRDS TO TALK

Teaching a parrot or mynah bird to talk can be an exciting adventure. You will want to begin early — before your bird is eighteen months old. Here are a few tips that you may want to follow.

First, before buying a bird in a store, ask the owner where the bird was

A blue and yellow macaw

born. This is important. If the bird was taken from its nest in the wild, it is best not to buy it. Today, many cockatoos and macaws are near extinction — due in part to the pet trade.

When you bring your pet home, give the bird a full day to get used to its new surroundings. It is important for a bird to feel safe and comfortable.

Give your pet a name. Usually a one- or two-syllable name, such as "Charlie" or "Polly," is easiest for a bird to remember. Repeat the name often. Then make a list of short phrases you would like your pet to learn — "pretty boy,"

A pair of budgies

"good girl," or "hello,
Charlie," "good night,
Polly." Use the phrases as
much as possible at times
when you want your pet to
say them to you. For

A pair of cockatiels

example, you should not
say "good night" in the
morning. Eventually, the
bird may say "good night"
just as you are going to

bed, because that's when you say it to your pet.

Always speak to your bird in a normal tone of voice — and be patient. You might spend at least half an hour each day repeating words and phrases that you want your bird to imitate. It may take weeks, or even months, before the training pays off. Remember that talking birds learn at different rates. If your bird has not learned to talk after about ten months, it may not be willing to talk at all.

If your bird learns quickly, try teaching it to sing a song. Above all, spend time with your pet. Every bird enjoys and needs exercise and attention. And remember to praise your pet's behavior with laughter and kind words. Rewarding your pet with food treats will also help.

Teaching your pet to talk can be an exciting adventure.

Learning to talk is a two-sided activity. For it to be worthwhile, both sides need to share time with and enjoy each other.

GLOSSARY

ability (a-BIL-it-ee) — natural talent or skill

affectionate (a-FEK-shuh-net) — showing a liking for a person or thing

captivity (kap-TIV-ih-tee) — kept within bounds or under control

chatter (CHAT-er) — short, quick sounds

communicate (kuh-MYOO-nuh-kayt) — to exchange information

contact calls (KAHN-takt KAWLS) — the calls that birds use to let members of the group know where they are

crest (KREST) — a showy tuft on the head of an animal

crown (KROWN) — the top of the head

duetting (doo-ET-ing) — two performers singing together

generation (jen-uh-RAY-shun) — a group of living things descended from the same ancestor

imitator (IM-uh-tayt-uhr) — one who copies another

instinctive (in-STINK-tiv) — natural ability that does not have to be learned

intruder (in-TROOD-er) — one who forces himself in

mate (MAYT) — to join as partners; to breed

mimic (MIM-ik) — to imitate

nape (NAYP) — the back of the neck

native people (NAYT-tiv PEE-puhl) — the people born in a certain region

nectar (NEK-ter) — a sweet liquid given off by plants

offspring (AWF-spring) — the young of an animal

organ (OR-gen) — a part of an animal that does a particular task

pollen (POHL-uhn) — the fine dust in a flower that fertilizes the seeds

predator (PREH-duh-tuhr) — an animal that kills and eats other animals

species (SPEE-sheez) — animals that form a distinct group made up of related individuals

syrinx (SIR-inks) — a highly developed organ for making sounds

talented (TAL-ent-ed) — to have unusual natural ability

territory (TEHR-uh-tohr-ee) — a geographical area belonging to an individual or group

trachea (TRAY-kee-a) — the tube that is used for breathing

unique (yoo-NEEK) — the only one of its kind

INDEX

(**Boldface** page numbers indicate illustrations.)

African gray
  parrots, 17, **17**,
  18, 20, **21**
Amazon parrots,
  18, 21–23
Australia, 6, **6**, 27,
  30, 34
Bald mynah birds,
  18
Blue and yellow
  macaws, **25, 39**
Budgies, 18, **18**,
  27–28, **28, 41**
Buying birds,
  38–40
Cayman amazon
  parrots, **21**
Central America, 4,
  21, 24, 28
Chattering lories, **34**
Cockatiels, 18, **32**,
  33, **42**
Cockatoos, 18,
  30–33, 39
Coleto mynah
  birds, **37**
Columbus,
  Christopher, 26
Common mynah
  birds, 18

Conures. **See**
  Parakeets
Crested larks, **8**
Crested mynah
  birds, 18
Crows, **7**
Double yellow-
  headed amazon
  parrot, 22
Duetting, 15
Endangered birds,
  39
Galah cockatoo, **31**
Golden-crested
  mynah birds, 18
Greater hill mynah
  birds, 16, 18,
  36–37
House mynah
  birds, 18
Human speech,
  6–7, 8, 13, 15, 16,
  36.
Hyacinth macaws,
  24, **25**
Indian hill mynah
  birds, **17, 18**
Javan Hill mynah
  birds, 18
Kea, **2**

Lesser hill mynah
  birds, 18, 36
Lories, 18, 34–35
Lorikeets, **4**, 18,
  34–35
Macaws, **4**, 18,
  24–26, 39, **39**
Military macaws, **25**
Mimicking, 5, 6–7,
  15, 16–19, 33, 36,
  37
Moluccan
  cockatoo, 30–31,
  31
Monk parakeets, **13**
Mynah birds, 5, 15,
  16, 17, **17**, 18, 19,
  36–37, 38
Northern
  mockingbirds, **10**
Parakeets, 12, **13**,
  18, 27–29, **45**
Parrots, **2, 4**, 5, 6,
  15, 16, 17, **17**, 18,
  19, 20-35, 36, 38
Pet trade, 39
Rainbow lorikeets,
  35, **35**
Red and yellow
  barbets, **14**

Red-collared
  lorikeets, **35**
Red-crowned
  parakeets, **29**
Rose-ringed
  parakeets, **29**
Scarlet macaws,
  25, 26
Singing, 5, 12–13,
  14, 15, 37, 44
Songbirds, 12, 17
South America, 4,
  21, 24, 28
Starlings, 6, **7**, 12,
  16, 36
Sun conures, **29**
Superb lyrebirds,
  6, **6**
Talk, teaching birds
  to, 38–45
Three-wattled
  bellbirds, **10**
Yellow-backed
  lories, **34**
Yellow-headed
  amazon parrots, **23**
Yellow-naped
  amazon parrots,
  22–23, **23**

ABOUT THE AUTHOR

Alice K. Flanagan is a freelance writer and bird advocate. She considers her strong interest in birds, and a feeling of kinship with them, a symbol of her independence and freedom as a writer. She enjoys writing, especially for children. "The experience of writing," she says, "is like opening a door for a caged bird, knowing you are the bird flying gloriously away."

Ms. Flanagan lives with her husband in Chicago, Illinois, where they take great pleasure in watching their backyard birds.